Apatosaurus

Aaron Carr

MIGHTY DINOSAURS

AV2

www.av2books.com

AV2

Step 1
Go to **www.av2books.com**

Step 2
Enter this unique code

QLANE56BE

Step 3
Explore your interactive eBook!

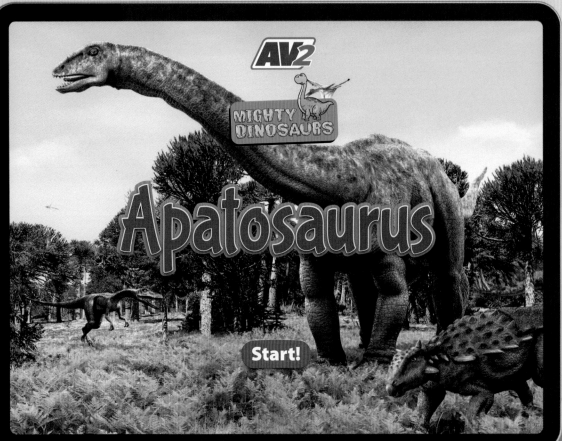

AV2

MIGHTY DINOSAURS

Apatosaurus

Start!

Your interactive eBook comes with...

Read							
	Audio Listen to the entire book read aloud	**Videos** Watch informative video clips	**Weblinks** Gain additional information for research	**Try This!** Complete activities and hands-on experiments	**Key Words** Study vocabulary, and complete a matching word activity	**Quizzes** Test your knowledge	**Slideshows** View images and captions

MIGHTY DINOSAURS

Apatosaurus

CONTENTS

3

Meet the Apatosaurus.

Its name means "deceptive lizard."

Apatosaurus was one of the largest animals to ever live on land.

It weighed more than 70,000 pounds.

Apatosaurus had a very long neck. It used its neck to reach food.

Apatosaurus was a plant eater.

It spent almost all of its time looking for food and eating.

Apatosaurus was one of the largest plant eaters ever to live.

Apatosaurus did not chew its food. It used its mouth and teeth to pull leaves off tree branches.

Apatosaurus walked very slowly on its four strong legs.

It may have also used its tail like an extra leg.

15

Apatosaurus lived in the middle part of North America.

It stayed far away from swamps and other watery places.

17

Apatosaurus died out more than 137 million years ago.

Apatosaurus fossils formed over millions of years.

The Carnegie Museum of Natural History in Pittsburgh has a nearly complete Apatosaurus fossil.

People can go to museums to learn more about the Apatosaurus.

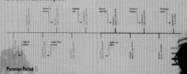

The Age of the Dinosaurs

Apatosaurus Facts

These pages provide detailed information that expands on the interesting facts found in the book. They are intended to be used by adults as a learning support to help young readers round out their knowledge of each amazing dinosaur or pterosaur featured in the *Mighty Dinosaurs* series.

Pages 4–5

Apatosaurus means "deceptive lizard." Apatosaurus is a massive dinosaur known for its long neck, huge body, and tail. For more than one hundred years, scientists believed that Apatosaurus and Brontosaurus were the same dinosaur. Apatosaurus was considered the proper name. In 2015, after researchers studied many different fossils, Brontosaurus was classified as a separate genus of dinosaur.

Pages 6–7

Apatosaurus was one of the largest animals to ever live on land. The Apatosaurus weighed as much as 80,000 pounds (36,000 kilograms). Measured from head to tail, the Apatosaurus was up to 70 feet (21 meters) long. Apatosaurus stood 15 feet (4.6 m) tall at the hip. The Apatosaurus was so large, scientists once thought it lived in water to support its weight.

Pages 8–9

Apatosaurus had a very long neck. Its neck was more than 17 feet (5 m) long. The Apatosaurus used its long neck to graze. Some scientists believe Apatosaurus could raise its head to eat leaves off high tree branches. Others say the extreme length of the neck would have prevented Apatosaurus from raising it more than 17 feet (5 m). Instead, the long neck would have allowed Apatosaurus to reach food in areas its huge body could not go, such as dense forests.

Pages 10–11

Apatosaurus was a herbivore, or plant eater. The Apatosaurus was one of the largest herbivores ever to live. In order to support its massive size, Apatosaurus would have spent nearly all of its time either searching for food or eating. Tree leaves, conifer seeds, and ferns were some of the plants Apatosaurus ate. Conifers were the dominant plants during the time period in which Apatosaurus lived, so they likely made up most of its diet.

Apatosaurus did not chew its food. The Apatosaurus used its peg-like teeth to strip leaves and conifer needles from tree branches. It did not use its teeth for chewing. Instead, the Apatosaurus swallowed its food whole. It also swallowed rocks, which stayed in the stomach and helped break down food. Some scientists think Apatosaurus may have had strong lips, like a moose, that would have helped it grasp its food.

Apatosaurus walked very slowly. The Apatosaurus had four huge legs shaped like thick columns. The front legs were slightly shorter than the hind legs. From studying preserved Apatosaurus tracks, scientists know that the dinosaur could only walk very slowly. However, Apatosaurus hatchlings could run quickly on their two hind legs. Some scientists also think Apatosaurus used its tail like a leg. This would have allowed Apatosaurus to stand up on its hind legs, using its tail for added support and balance.

Apatosaurus lived in the middle part of North America. The Apatosaurus lived in both North America and Europe. In North America, Apatosaurus was found in the middle part of the continent, in the present-day states of Colorado, Utah, Wyoming, and Oklahoma. The massive size of the Apatosaurus meant that it had to live far away from swamps and large bodies of water. This is because it would have sank into the soft ground in these areas.

Apatosaurus died out more than 137 million years ago during the Late Jurassic Period. People learned about the Apatosaurus from studying its fossils. Fossils are formed when an animal dies and is quickly covered in sand, mud, or water. This keeps the hard parts of the body, such as bones, teeth, and claws, from decomposing. The body is pressed between layers of mud and sand. Over millions of years, the layers turn into stone, and the dinosaur's bones and teeth turn into stone as well. This preserves the size and shape of the dinosaur.

People can go to museums to learn more about the Apatosaurus. People from all around the world visit museums each year to see Apatosaurus fossils in person. Not many Apatosaurus fossils have been found, and most of those are incomplete. The Carnegie Museum of Natural History in Pittsburgh, Pennsylvania, has a nearly complete Apatosaurus skeleton with a skull. It was discovered in 1909.

KEY WORDS

Research has shown that as much as 65 percent of all written material published in English is made up of 300 words. These 300 words cannot be taught using pictures or learned by sounding them out. They must be recognized by sight. This book contains 55 common sight words to help young readers improve their reading fluency and comprehension. This book also teaches young readers several important content words, such as proper nouns. These words are paired with pictures to aid in learning and improve understanding.

Page	Sight Words First Appearance	Page	Content Words First Appearance
4	its, means, name, the	4	Apatosaurus, lizard
6	animals, land, live, of, on, one, to, was	7	pounds
7	it, more, than	9	neck
9	a, food, had, long, used, very	10	plant eater
10	all, almost, and, for, plant, time	12	branches, mouth, teeth
12	did, leaves, not, off, tree	14	legs, tail
14	also, an, four, have, like, may, walked	16	North America
16	in, part	17	swamps
17	away, far, from, other, places	19	fossils
18	out, years	20	Carnegie Museum of Natural History, Pittsburgh
19	over	21	museums
20	has		
21	about, can, go, learn, people		

Published by AV2
350 5th Avenue, 59th Floor
New York, NY 10118
Website: www.av2books.com

Library of Congress Control Number: 2019950184

ISBN 978-1-7911-1656-9 (hardcover)
ISBN 978-1-7911-1657-6 (softcover)
ISBN 978-1-7911-1658-3 (multi-user eBook)

Printed in Guangzhou, China
1 2 3 4 5 6 7 8 9 0   24 23 22 21 20

022020
100919

Project Coordinator: Priyanka Das
Art Director: Terry Paulhus

Every reasonable effort has been made to trace ownership and to obtain permission to reprint copyright material. The publishers would be pleased to have any errors or omissions brought to their attention so that they may be corrected in subsequent printings.

All illustrations by Jon Hughes, pixel-shack.com. AV2 acknowledges Alamy, Dreamstime, Getty, and Shutterstock as its primary image suppliers for this title.